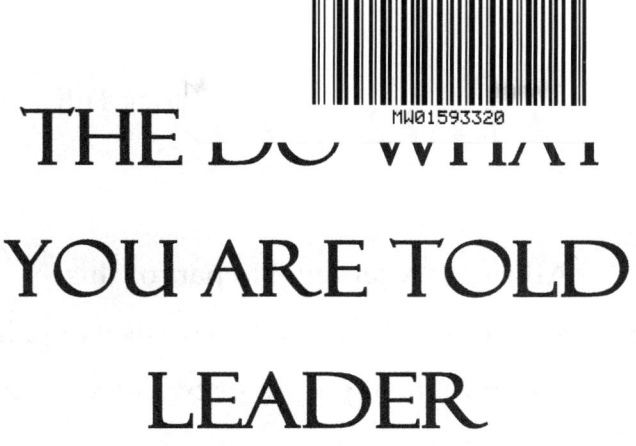

# THE DO WHAT
# YOU ARE TOLD
# LEADER

## Shagdrick Hill

Published by Writers of the West
Printed in United States of America

*"The Do What You're Told Leader"* Is dedicated to Jesus, who has been an amazing teacher and the best big brother anyone could ever ask for. He has been the example I needed in life in every aspect one could imagine. He has shown me what it truly means to be an example of how I should be *'About My Father's Business.'*

I just want to thank you for sacrificing your life so that I can live and be a servant.

# Table of Contents

*Lord, thank you for the opportunity to gain wisdom and knowledge through one of your other vessels, as I begin this journey of reading "The Do What You Are Told Leader." I ask that the words and illustrations in this book be something I am able to apply and use in my daily life, as I desire to lead others according to your will.*

# 1

# Introduction

Let's have a conversation about the real reason I wrote this book. As you read, you will hear about some of my real-life experiences and how I overcame them, whether they came from happy moments or a place of darkness. They all contributed to shaping the leader and motivator I am today. The title of this book comes from my journey as a leader, not having a sense of direction or experience, yet knowing I was a leader. This is also the reason behind naming and developing each chapter.

I knew life was supposed to be better than what it was at the time. I believed that God had so much more in store for me than what I was experiencing. One of my real motivations came from a comment that was shared with me about myself. I carry this comment with me, not in a negative way, but as a reminder of my humble beginnings and the drive it sparked within me. The comment was, "He's young and smart; it seems like he knows it all, but why should I listen to him? He doesn't have anything." Man, that was a real eye-opener for me. It didn't make me focus on acquiring material possessions but rather on how people might dismiss my advice due to my age or my perceived lack of experience in a given situation.

This comment drove me on a quest for even more knowledge and information than ever before. I began reading every leadership book I felt God put me in a position to read. I am a firm believer in learning from other people's mistakes and experiences. I see it as if they've already gone through and are willing to share what they've learned during their lifetime. Now, I have the opportunity to gain from their wisdom and experience, with God as the ultimate teacher, through "LIFE." I can receive a portion of their time spent here on Earth, which probably took them years of learning, within a matter of hours just by reading their books. All I can say is, "Let me make a reservation to read that book."

I also went on to gain more experience in leadership roles, whether it was for less pay or, in some cases, no pay at all. I did it not only for myself but also for all of you. I knew that through my sacrifice, I would one day be able to share my experiences to help you and others like you achieve the success you desire in the field of leadership.

Now I am no expert, but what I do know is the wisdom and knowledge that's on the inside of this book will help you succeed in your daily life as well as in your professional leadership roles. I also know being a leader is something that each of us has on the inside and I defiantly can help you draw on that ability to lead people. I need you to want to be successful for yourself. Others may truly want you to accomplish your dreams and goals, but until you want it for yourself they will never happen. The moment I took ownership for my life and all the responsibilities that came along with it is when life began to change.

None of us will lead the exact same way, but the core principles and foundation of leadership are all the same. It's when you add your personality and experiences that makes your style of leadership unique. Your audience or team members will respond rather it is in a positive or negative manner. There will be times when you will transition into leadership roles and you have to decide the direction you want to move with your team. I will also go into further details about this in a later chapter of this book.

Overall while going through this material I need you to take ownership and responsibility of you, because leadership starts with you. It's impossible to lead someone else if you can't lead yourself, so let's continue this conversation in *"Walk the Line and Don't Cross It."*

*Lord, I ask for the ability to continuously walk in integrity and take ownership of all my actions and responsibilities as I serve as a vessel for others to witness my ability to lead and guide them. I also ask for your strength and encouragement, knowing that there may be times when I am presented with challenges. However, with your help, I am confident that I can "Walk the Line and Don't Cross It.*

# 2

# Walk the Line and Don't Cross It

We are here to talk about leadership, but being a leader first starts with being human. Being a leader is having a personal Code of Conduct. We will get into business and how to lead as you continue to read the chapters to come, but none of it matters if you don't have a personal Code of Conduct.

You as the leader must have a sense of direction of what you want for yourself and your future. (People without vision perish Proverb 29:18.) Simply put you must have integrity. I like to define integrity as a person who is honest with the characteristics of holding their values even during times of distress or adversities. Basically, you must have the ability to do as the title says "Walk the Line and Don't Cross It". I don't expect you to be perfect, because even Jesus disciples had flaws. As a leader your team better know you have this one major characteristic otherwise, they won't follow. Those that do follow you I would advise you to get rid of them because they don't have integrity neither thus eliminating your team.

The reason I say integrity by far is the most important characteristic is, because if you can follow the directions of this title during any situation you have just accomplished two things. One your team knows no matter the circumstance you as the leader will guide them and standup for them no matter the cause. The second thing this does is shows God that you are trustworthy and He can give you more because of it.

Think about it for yourself the more you trust a person the more responsibility you give them, because you trust they are going to do the right thing at all times and get the job done. According to your Code of Conduct. On the flip side as the leader when time for advancement or something that gives that person a reward you are going to give it to them, because you trust them. You feel as they have earned the advancement or the reward that is due to their loyalty to serve as a member of the team with such a high level of integrity.

Imagine being on an elliptical machine getting your workout for the day. There is a row of pennies in front of the machine, but as you take your steps on the machine that is allowing you to reach your work out goal. You find that it is very difficult to do both as a result you can't get to the pennies. Now a decision must be made. Either walk the line and not cross it or step off to gather the pennies.

Decision One allows you to reach your goal with a little hard work and perseverance.

While Decision Two allows you to get off bend down and gain some pennies. This is what happens in life when you cross the line. You feel as if you gained some pennies and you have achieved something. Whereas the keyword here was PENNIES. I don't care if it was billions of dollars you earned while stepping off track in Gods eyes it was only pennies. As a result you now have to live with the guilt and the pain of your actions. Knowing you gained something the wrong way and it is not protected or covered under Gods law.

I started earlier by stating you should have a personal Code of Conduct. I will give you a couple of nuggets I have within mine. Starting with integrity which we won't go into since we have been talking about that this chapter. Next would be being a person of your word. Simply put do what you say you are going to do and simply do it. If for some reason you can't do what it is you agreed to do "Say it", so the proper arrangements can be made. Next would be to value the time that is given to you and don't waste it doing foolish things. Time is the one thing that puts us all on an equal playing field. I encourage you to begin to distance yourself when you have people who believe in wasting not only their time, but others around them as well. Have people on your team who respect and value their time, because they understand while working the task at hand, we need to get this done as quickly but as effectively as possible.

You also will hear this as "Working smarter not harder or getting more done within less time." I am sure none of us wakes up in the morning and say, "I just want to do a lot of work today?" No, but we understand that in order to enjoy the fruits of our labor there has to be some sort of labor done for us to enjoy those fruits. One last nugget, but by far the most important seek higher powers take the time to pray and communicate to God. He is the map eventually in life I will go over this in detail, but for now know that He is the map and the best way to get to where you are going is by looking at the map.

I can't tell you how often in life we wonder why we are not where we are supposed to be in life. The answer is quiet simple we never go to the map or when we do go we are so far off course that we expect a miracle to happen to put us where we want to be. When the truth of the matter is we want microwave blessing when we mess up and not have to suffer any of the hardships that come along with our poor decision-making process at the time. Here is a secret God does issue out microwave blessings on His time not ours. (2 Peter 3:8) Developing that personal relationship with God can put you light years ahead of your time. If you simply develop the relationship with Him and "Walk the Line and Don't Cross It"

*Lord, now that you have placed me in this position, I trust and lean on you for your guidance, as I know you have a plan for the sheep you have allowed me to shepherd. I ask that you use me in this role as a beacon of hope for those who desire to embark on the journey of leadership. We all must, at some point, begin in the "Here" position.*

# 3

# You Are Here But You Need To Be There

Starting a position of leadership is only the beginning. There's nothing like having a boss who is inexperienced. When starting off, you want to take the time to know your employees or coworkers. Being "There" is when you've climbed the ladder to reach your desired position or dream. While doing so, you were still able to earn the respect of your employees and coworkers, maintaining a high level of functionality. This is why you hold your position.

Being "Here" is not a bad position to be in. In fact, all leaders have been in this position at some point in their lives or careers. The goal is not to get discouraged, but to embrace the moment. Believe it or not, when you look back at your past, this will be one of your most cherished moments in life, which you will share with others currently in the "Here" position. Obviously, there's something inside you that was recognized, putting you in the "Here" position.

Whether you've been climbing the ladder to reach this level or if favor has landed you the position, you're "Here," and we're going to make the best of it.

The first thing you want to do is understand the pieces of the puzzle you have (which we will discuss in more detail later). Study your team's profiles to find out their achievements, both in terms of career and personal goals, and whether they have families. You might wonder why this is important to you. Let me inform you that there's nothing like having a team member who wants your job. This is fine if you know how to channel their energy in the right direction—supporting the team's mission and the task at hand. You always want team members whose goal is to achieve more for themselves and the team.

As the leader, this benefits your team because they'll be willing to continue their job education on the path to success, driven by their personal goals and dreams. What you don't need is someone trying to sabotage your job or team. If you're unaware of a mole and their intentions for damaging your team, it can be very stressful. You need to find out if the team member plans to stay long term or if this is just a job until another one comes along. They might even be an outsider placed in an office where they won't perform at their highest level.

Their personal goals are equally important because a great leader cares for their personnel as a whole (I'm not saying you should interfere into their personal business; you're not trying to make them your best friend). You're building and establishing a relationship, which wfe'll discuss further as you continue reading. You need to know about their past achievements because, as a leader, you want leaders under you, fitting the title "The Do What You Are Told Leader."

For years, I wasn't placed in a position of authority; I observed and learned. People told me what to do and when to do it. I realize this sounds harsh, but it's true. I knew I was a leader, but I didn't know how to get there, so I took the next best step. I sought information and experience, sacrificing for it.

I understood that leadership was more than just a fancy title; it was part of who I was inside and out. Eventually, I would use this information and experience to become a great leader, as I shared with you earlier.

After reviewing their profiles and discovering more about them, you should have a thorough understanding of each position under your leadership. Learn what these positions require. The next step is to hold a team meeting. This allows you to set the team's mood. You provide them with a vision (Habakkuk 2:2) of where they're headed as long as they're part of the team. A leader without vision is a leader who's going nowhere, and going there fast. In other words, if a leader doesn't know the direction to lead their people, why are they leading? People respect someone who knows their life's direction, and they tend to work harder, wanting to be there with their leader to prove their worthiness. (The key to a great team is a strong foundation, which starts at the beginning of the relationship.)

In this meeting, you may pass out a handout asking them some of those questions discussed earlier, because you may not be able to sit and meet with each one of them individually. This meeting defines who you are as a leader. You want to relay that over to your team. This outlines what you expect from them and how you expect them to carry themselves as members of the team. You are laying the foundation.

Being in the "Here" position requires you to have a backbone. Believe me when I tell you that your team is going to test you by seeing how far you are going to let them go before you decide you are going to do something about it. You are laying the foundation for things to come. That was my third time saying, "You are laying the foundation," because I really need you to know and understand how important this step is for you right now in the "Here" position.

For example, this is how I would host the meeting: The first thing I would do is introduce myself and then proceed with giving just a brief history of myself. Next, I would inform them of the values that will be implemented while I am at the helm. I would then share the vision and the goal expectations moving forward. I would also explain what would not be tolerated while performing as team members, both at work and away from work. This is because if they perform poorly in their personal lives away from work, they run the risk of not being at their best while at work, thus compromising the team's overall success. In closing the meeting, I would encourage everyone to quickly fill out and return the handout.

Before I open the floor for any type of questions, I would stress the importance of following the guidelines that have been put into place, explaining how doing so will result in great success at work and at home. Failure to do so will lead to either verbal or written warnings, and if not corrected, could result in termination of their duties. Then, I would allow them to ask questions, as you need to be a leader who is reachable and allows them to voice their concerns. In other words, your team needs to feel a connection coming from your position of authority; it lets them know you are the leader, but you are human as well and can be communicated with.

Now, allow me to go into further detail about why I would like to know some of their personal goals and career aspirations. As a leader, you are there to shepherd the people under you (1 Peter 5:2). Knowing a person's personal goals, for one, lets them know you take an interest in them. Secondly, when an opportunity arises, you may be able to help that person achieve a goal, which in return will motivate them to work harder for you. This is because you went out of your way to help them accomplish something that was personal to them. Knowing their career goals will allow you to see where they want to be in the future, and you can help guide them down the right path. Just as you want to continue to rise and move up the ladder, so do your team members.

As a good leader, you should be looking for that person who will lead your team after you leave that position. It's important to know whether or not they have a family because, let's be honest, there is more at risk for them than for someone who doesn't. Besides, it's a long drive home when you have to tell your spouse that you no longer have a job. I've been in that position, and it's not a good feeling.

When you have a family, you're going to respect that job a little bit more because you have a responsibility to keep putting food on the table and a roof over your family's head.

You need to know each job description inside out. This will help you in the future; if there's a problem, you'll quickly be able to identify who was responsible for it. It will also save time when doing evaluations. You can read reports, see how the company is excelling, and quickly identify the position responsible for the rise on the charts.

Let's recap what we've learned so far in this chapter. We started by understanding that we are in a "Here" position. We began to grasp the importance of conducting a brief background check on our team's career and personal goals, whether they have a family, or even if they plan on staying with the company long-term. We walked through the significance of laying the foundation of your leadership while guiding the team toward the vision at hand. We gained a better understanding of why we should be familiar with the duties of each position they will perform. We even had an example of how we should host a meeting and convey our thoughts to our team members so they know what to expect while performing their job duties at work. Lastly, we learned how we need to be reachable from our position of authority.

*Lord, I ask you for wisdom in selecting and placing the pieces of this puzzle. I understand you use me as a picture during this moment of team building, as we all pull hand over hand to prepare this boat for the deep blue seas ahead.*

# 4

# A Puzzle Needs Pieces

Knowing who you have around will help your overall success; thus, the title "A Puzzle Needs Pieces." A completed puzzle forms a picture, and once the puzzle is held up at a distance, you don't see all of the pieces that made the picture; your focus is the picture as a whole. What this means is that you should know whether you are a picture or a piece, but understand that you can't be both while working on a project. A piece is someone who knows and understands their position and the value they hold as a piece. A picture is the leader; they are the ones who have all the attention and focus on them, yet they understand that there are pieces that made them the picture. Understanding this metaphor will help you decide who goes where and when they are to be there.

We touched on this briefly while reading "You Are Here But You Need To be There" in an earlier chapter. Now that we have an understanding that you are a leader, you should understand that you are the picture for your team. The goal now is to put the proper pieces together so that the puzzle can be formed.

There are two types of puzzles we are going to work with in this reading. The first one is the one when you buy a puzzle and you open it up, and you just kind of dump all of the pieces out onto where you are going to be putting the puzzle together. This type of puzzle, you just work with the pieces that were given. You understand they were inside the box, and you know they will form a picture when it's all said and done.

That's just like when you take on the "Here" position. Allow me to give you a topic you can relate to. It's like the President when they are elected into office, and now they have to take on the responsibilities the prior President left for them. Some of them would say they have to clean up the mess that we are in, so they just have to work with the pieces that are already in place. They know where they want to lead us, and they have a picture of the outcome. As long as they continue to work, the picture will come together.

Now, remember you are in the "Here" position. You have all these pieces scattered around, but you've got a vision (a box on what it should look like). The first thing you do is look at the box because you are getting that picture stored on the inside of your brain. Next, you begin moving around the pieces so that you can see what you have. You also want to identify and find the four corners of the puzzle. Then you want to put the pieces together that have the same colors with them because you're looking at the picture, and you know they go with one another or the ones that will go around the edges.

By doing this, what you have actually done is broken the puzzle up into sections, which now makes it easier to manage. A wise person never tries to put the puzzle together in just one piece. They work the puzzle in sections, then they put the sections together to form the picture.

Now, while you were reading that, I was working on a system so that you would have a clear understanding of the illustration at hand. Let's go back and break everything down in detail. First, we had to look at the box so that you could get the picture stored on the inside of your brain. What this meant was you, as the leader, look at the full picture. This may be the goal at hand, also called the vision. You need this on the inside of you so that no matter what goes on or how hard it may be, you have a clear understanding of where you are going.

Next, you moved the pieces around to see what you had in front of you. What this is, is you start checking those profiles, getting to know their history, the things we discussed earlier. You walk and go inside their workstations; you find as much information about them as you can. Our next step was identifying the four corners of the puzzle. This is one of the most important pieces because here is where you are going to find some team leaders—someone who you can go to on behalf of the section they're over.

Could you imagine having 500 people under you, trying to manage them all? You would lose your mind (Exodus 18:13-27). It is easier to go to the team leaders and hold smaller meetings with them than to try and get all 500 together at one time. Next, there was you matching the pieces that had the same colors together or go around the edges together. What this caused was you knowing the job descriptions, knowing the profiles of the team member, and knowing your team leaders so that you could place them in the proper section.

Then I closed with the wise man not doing the puzzle in one piece but breaking it into sections because it's easier to take all of the matching sections and begin putting the puzzle together in sections rather than pieces. Before you know it, you would have put the whole puzzle together to form the whole picture.

In leadership, you must have people you can count on, which is the reason for the team leaders. Team leaders then help you manage the rest of the team. Now, if for some unexpected reason, there is a problem, you, as the leader, will take the blame because all eyes are on you and not the team leaders or the rest of the team. You never want to throw your team members under the bus if you plan on having them around long.

Now, if you have come to the conclusion that their services are no longer needed, you still let them go with some form of class. You don't just yell at them and tell them they are fired. Remember, they are still God's children, and what goes up must come down. Also, you still have other team members who would be witnesses to you being disrespectful and mismanaging the team. This would then paint the picture that if you did it to that member of the team, you would do it to them as well. Which could result in them not wanting to be on your team any longer? Once that occurs, all of your hard work that you have done to put the process in order for the team in place would be thrown out the window, so again I say if that person is no longer needed on the team and you feel it is time for them to go, do so with some form of class.

The second form of putting together a puzzle is in the form of you picking your pieces to get to the end result of the picture you have in mind. Since earlier we were talking about the President, I am going to stay in that same vein as I paint a different picture. Once the President is elected, he has to play on the field that has been chosen for him, but it doesn't mean he can't choose his players. The President then starts to put together his executive office, like the Vice President and so on. This brings me to how I am going to illustrate this second puzzle. I am sure some of you have played in a pickup game of football or basketball, maybe even some baseball. I know I have, and it actually brought about a lot of fun and excitement as a child. Getting out there to compete against others and allowing your skills to be put on display.

Well, allow me to refresh your memory. It first starts with electing a captain of the team, and then they proceed to make their picks until the team is formed. Now, as captain, it's your job to put together the best team as possible to win the game. With that come decisions from the captain, such as looking at the players to see if they are in shape or what type of gear they have on. Or even asking a question like "Can you catch or how fast are you?" These decisions and questions are important because they have the vision to get their team to victory, and they want to make sure they choose the best players possible.

Now, once the game starts, the ball will be in the hands of the players who they know will produce the plays needed to win. Now, while this game is going on, the captain is still giving the ball to some of those other players because they are seeing who they will be able to depend on in the future or whether or not they need to allow them to be on the team for next time. When it's all said and done, and the team has taken its victory and the captain is elected MVP, now the eyes are on them because they took the most risk. Now, what does this mean is the question I know you are asking.

When that captain was first elected captain, they had to do some research. They had to look to see who was out on that field ready to play. What that simply was, as a leader, you were stepping into a position of authority and you were building the company from the ground up. You needed to know whose resumes were out in the market. While determining whose resumes were out in the market, you were asking those questions, "Can you catch" or "How fast are you" In other words, you were asking if they had a degree or how much experience they had.

Once your team was selected and the game got going, you went to the ones who had that degree or the experience because you knew they could produce what you needed to run the company. As stated, you didn't just go to them every time, though. You gave those who didn't have a degree or the experience the opportunity because we are in America, the land of opportunity.

We all know in the real world, starting a company, you won't just get all of the top performers. As a leader, you are going to have to look at a person and see whether or not they have the potential for them to be what you need. Which is why you still let them have the ball and try to make plays because in the future, those will be the individuals who step up into that leadership role if you plan for your company to not hit that plateau but continue to peak.

When it is all said and done, they are looking at the CEO of that company and how they have reached such a high level. The world won't see all those hardworking people that got the company up to the top just as in football, they don't see those offensive linemen with those fantastic blocks. But as a leader, it's your job to go back and tell your guys, "Good job, nice work out there today." When it boils down to it, as a leader, knowing every piece of the puzzle is very valuable if you want to be able to put that puzzle together.

Knowing whether or not, going into a relationship, you are a piece or a picture is also important. You don't want two pictures in the same puzzle; it won't work. There will be a lot of head-butting going on, and one will have to leave. Knowing when to be the picture and when to be a piece is valuable information as well. There are times when you will be working on projects, and you need to be that piece and not that picture; it doesn't make you any less of a leader. Normally, when leaders come together, they all understand the whole picture of the puzzle at hand.

This is why you're reading this book, "The Do What You Are Told Leader." Leaders know when to be submissive to carry out a plan from the leader who, at the time, is the picture. Why is it easier for them during this time to let go of their leadership role and become a piece? It's because, at that moment, that leader knows the vision and they are willing to submit to their leadership to carry out the vision.

Let's do a quick recap of what we learned in this chapter. We learned the lesson of putting together two types of puzzles: one was when we just dumped the puzzle out and we put the pieces together. We used team leaders because it's faster to put together the puzzle if we do it in sections, then bring it all together. Secondly, we learned about the captain who built the company from the ground up and how the decisions they make will lead the company to victory. Lastly, we learned how to be a piece even when we are a picture to get the vision done.

*Lord, I thank you for the ability to open and use all of my senses as you place me in the driver seat as you prepare the blades for the harvest for your server's fruits of their labor. Although we are not "There" yet we thank you for what you have already done.*

# 5

# Listening Requires More Than Your Ears

You can understand more of the message if you focus on everything being said. Body language plays a major role in what is being said. Ever heard the term 'actions speak louder than words'? This is true because if a person shows up late to work every day and you ask them, 'Would they like to keep their job?' and they continue to show up late, they are telling you they don't want their job because they continue to come in late. This indicates they don't value their job enough to come to work on time. Using all of your senses will help you understand what is going on in your environment and how you should handle the situation.

Listening requires more than your ears; it allows you to really get involved with your team members, whether you're leading from the bottom or you're the head leader. This type of listening requires focus on your behalf. 'Attention to detail' is what I was told during my early days in the United States Navy. What they were simply telling me was to focus on what it was I was doing, otherwise I would be right back doing the same thing tomorrow or until I get it right. The more I thought about it, the more I understood what it was they were telling me. They were training me to notice everything; every little detail matters.

While serving my country in those days really molded me to become sharp with my eyes. It wasn't until one of my supervisors pulled me aside and instilled wisdom inside of me, which I will keep until it's time for me to move on. The wisdom was, 'As long as you have a sharp uniform and a clean workspace, no one will ever bother you.' Now you are wondering how or why this is a great piece of advice? Well, allow me to share why I felt this was great advice. People see you even when you don't see them; they are watching you perform or live your daily life. With this advice, I did two things with it.

One was to find something on that boat nobody cared about that was important, but nobody wanted to mess with. The second was to have a uniform so clean that when I walked by, you noticed its perfection. What I found for goal one was the capstan. We would use the capstan when coming in and out of port. This piece of equipment helped us hold the line (rope) once we got the line around it. This was a very important piece of equipment. The only problem with it was it was rusty on its sides where the line would go, and on the top, it was very dull due to all of the saltwater being splashed on it over time.

I remember when I first began to work on remodeling this project; it was rough because the sides had to be sanded down and oiled. As for the top, to get rid of the dullness, I would have to use Never Dull to get this gold to shine to its full ability. It would take me a week because it had been mistreated, left uncovered for months, and all of the saltwater built onto it and would have to come off. So for the next week, I worked very hard, sanding down the sides and using the Never Dull to get it back shiny.

For the next year and a half, every day I came to work, I would sand and shine it to keep it looking great. The guys in my division began to take notice, and when they walked by, they would slap it as if it was a female's bottom. This all was important because even when I was away on leave, they would clean it for me, because now something that looked as if it was nothing began to show its value once a little time was put into it.

The second goal was to get my uniform in the shape of perfection. What I did was start with my boots. I bought new ones. I found someone who I respected and asked about their boots and where they got them from. There were two people on my whole ship who had these boots, and one happened to be one of my BM1's (Boats Mate). But what I noticed about him was he had a very special boot; that shine was greater than any other shine I had seen before. I talked to him, found out where I could buy me a pair. Now these boots were expensive, but I knew if I wanted to achieve my goal, I would need those boots. Secondly, I bought new uniforms and had them dry-cleaned.

Next was the second person that had those boots, a gentleman who was 7 to 8 yrs my senior, but easier to relate to and I could see how everyone respected him; he was a

SH2. What caught my attention was the boots; more importantly, it was his uniform. The uniform was neat, he was well-groomed, and his work ethic was outstanding, yet he made it look so simple. He would then show me the ropes, but on a much bigger scale. He would mentor me, but I had to be smart enough to catch on and not stop his progression as he climbed the ladder as well.

The last person on this list was a guy who was also 7 to 8 yrs my senior; he also was well-groomed (Petty Officer). He taught me the products to buy and how to handle myself away from work and still have fun. I mention these three guys because with their help, my goal was achieved. I not only had the best uniform in my division, my work ethic was already there but they made me better, and along with it, my physical appearance and self-confidence all increased.

I told you these things because they were basic things that I watched, and if you do the same, it will build your esteem and get people to look at you who might not have if you hadn't listened with your eyes. As mentioned before, you can also listen through a person's actions. I gave you a practical example in which you could follow so that you are aware when you're leading.

Let's look at how paying attention to detail can also be another part of listening. I am sure you have heard the term "Time is money," but have you paid attention to why this is said? It's said because maintaining and following a schedule at times can be very difficult, and the last thing you need is for a person not to respect it.

We will stay in the same vein as our earlier example with the person showing up late. Not only did he show you he had no respect for his job, but the time lost can be significant. Time lost can result in lost profits if he is someone responsible on a product line. The product line cannot run if they are missing. A product line that is not running is a product line that is not producing a profit. This puts the company behind schedule, especially if the product needed to be shipped because now it doesn't ship, and you have an angry customer on the other end who has an angry customer on their end, all because you have a person who fails to come to work on time.

Actions from a leader can cause major results from the people around you to function better within the company. When a leader steps out with confidence, the members of the team notice. They are more likely to work harder than before. They're listening with their eyes through the leader's actions. Remember when we talked about how you should come in and lay down what will happen from here on out once you became the leader and you held a meeting? Well, the team is now focusing on how you behave as well. If you demanded that they be on time, they're watching to see if you are on time as well. You also want to make sure that the proper technology is in place so that each member can do their job properly. I am not saying go out and buy the most expensive equipment on the market. What I am saying is if you have a bus driver who has been driving and has a clean record, reward them with one of the newer buses. Don't have them driving the ones that break down all the time. It's important when you are a leader and you are listening with more than your ears that you make sure you walk in integrity because integrity will carry you a long way in your career.

I started this chapter off with the story of how I would clean the capstan along with going and finding the individuals needed to push me to the next level I was looking for. I want to break down exactly what was happening while this was going on so you can see how I was listening with more than just my ears at the time.

The significance of cleaning the capstan was truly a joy and a blessing for me. Even to this day, I need that quiet time in the mornings to think, and that's what this assignment allowed me to do. What most people didn't realize about that piece of equipment was when the captain of our ship sat on the bridge (the top part of the ship where the driving of the ship takes place) and looked out of the window, the first thing he would see is the capstan. The reason being is you have this big gold plate, and when the sun hits it, it sends off a shiny reflection. So, for a long period of time, there was no reflection because no one took pride in it. Now, he has this reflection hitting him in the face every time he goes to sit in his captain's chair. Over time, he sends someone to thank the department for a job well done on keeping our ship in excellence. As a result, my supervisors take notice of me. All the while, I have been learning and following people of leadership and staying in excellence.

One day, my BM1 comes to me saying, "At this time, have this uniform on and meet me on the forward deck" (the front half of the ship). Once I arrived there, I was told to line up and stand, and within a matter of minutes, the captain of the ship comes and rewards me with a NAM (Navy Achievement Medal). At the time, this was important because people my age (18) and people with my rank (E3) did not achieve this award; it was unheard of. In fact, when I wore my uniform with the medal on it, people would stop and look at me in disbelief.

I chose to go after better and listen with more than just my ears. It caused me to rise among my peers, but most importantly, respect was shown when I asked someone to do something for me in my role of leadership. Listening with more than just your ears will play a significant role for you while in the leadership position. You have to be willing to allow what God has given you in all of your senses to guide you while you are leading.

Always remember you are what's attracted to you. The type of person you are will be drawn to you, and it is your job to observe and use those senses that have been given to you to make the right decisions for the people you're leading.

*Lord I believe you have allowed me to take the steps to put my feet on the ground towards the finish line of green pastures and I am aware of the times you held me in positions to watch and observe others. As you would teach me to be patient so that I could learn and be prepared for the position I am currently in.*

# 6

# Listen From The Bottom Up

You learned many things along the way, and sometimes you have to go back to when you were at the bottom and remember all of those things that would cause you to say, "If I was the boss, I would do this. Or if I was the leader, I would have done that like this." When you allow yourself to go back to where motivation and the position you are now in were first created, what this does is allow you to become connectable. People listen to those they can connect with. They tend to work harder for someone they feel understands them.

Once you have made it to your position, you will then find someone in a higher position than you and continue to work from the bottom up, because motivation will continue to drive you in a higher direction. Understanding this principle will allow you to always be teachable. A leader who is willing to learn is a leader who is willing to lead. All that simply means is that a leader who is willing to listen and learn from others is worth following. Nobody wants to follow a person who thinks they know it all. Remember in the Introduction, this was something that happened to me. I chose not to get discouraged, but rather use it as a motivational tool to help me become a better leader and person as a whole.

This will be an exciting chapter because you will have to take some time out to look into your past and remember some of those thoughts that motivated you to push forward to get you in the position of leadership you are now in. One of the first things I would like you to do is get yourself a notebook or a piece of paper, so that you can write down some of your thoughts on this matter. I have been doing this for years on every little thing that I do. I find it to be very useful when strategically planning to brainstorm.

When you allow yourself to go back and draw up these thoughts and experiences that had once occurred, you will find yourself critiquing your past life. What this does is allows you to correct mistakes and then you strategically react out what was said or done on paper. There is power in putting information on paper. The power comes because now you are taking ownership of what you may have made a mistake on, which opens the door to ask for forgiveness if need be.

Now let me be clear, I am not asking you to go to individuals and ask for forgiveness if that is one of the things you put on your paper that you feel you made a mistake on, because depending on the issue, people can be not so forgiving. It's best that you take some issues to God because He knows your heart, so allow Him to work and change the hearts of others.

Even as a leader, we don't have those sorts of powers to change what's on the inside of people that might have caused them some sort of issues. On that paper, if you are younger and have never been in a position of leadership, and this is your first leadership role, I want you to do a timeline dating back to the start of the position you were in before you became a leader. Those of you who have been in leadership positions prior to this leadership position, I would like you as well to do a timeline on leadership positions you have been in and how they started and ended.

Depending on how they ended, look at some of the strengths and weaknesses that might have occurred during that role. For example, if a weakness for the assignment was you may have become too close to those you were leading and for some reason when it came time for them to follow your lead, they chose to do it their way. This is something that happens in leadership roles quite often, especially in cases when you were in the same position as them and then you are promoted to a position of authority. Here is where you have to separate yourself from that old position. Understand you are the same person, but your responsibilities have changed. If you want to remain in that role of leadership, you have to take those new responsibilities seriously.

For those of you reading this book and you have never been in any position of leadership, but you want to be in the future, I would like for you to keep your notepad close by. As I give my demonstration, I would like you to take notes and email me your response to what you think I should have done as a leader, and in return, I will share with you my response on the correction I made once I went and sought counsel on the situation.

In one of my first leadership roles, part of it was to introduce myself, show the new person what it was they would be doing on a daily basis, and what was expected of them. What I did was just that; I introduced myself and showed them around the facility. I informed them I once was in the position they were currently in. I befriended them so they understood we are one in the same; if you need something, never hesitate to ask, I am more than happy to help you so that you can perform your job on a high level. Once we made it back to the workstation they would be working, I proceeded with showing them the entire task they would be expected to do. (I have a belief that once you go into someone else's territory, you allow them to show you how it is they do things, because you may think that you know, but if you never worked for them before, you don't know how it is they want it until they tell you.)

Later, I then allowed them to do the task while I monitored their work. I felt as if this would be a good opportunity for them to ask questions as we went on, as sometimes questions arise during the actual hands-on training. I feel that this is a good strategy because individuals don't know what questions to ask if they have never worked in that type of environment until real-life situations start to occur, and the only way this happens is through practice. Once their shift was over, I simply let them know this is what they would be doing, and if they had any questions, please feel free to ask. How do you feel the training went?

Remember in this chapter, we learned that reflection can be the best motivator and teacher. Take time to reflect on what got you to where you are today and all of those old emotions to help make you more relatable for those who are in positions below you that you may lead. Also, being too relatable or reachable may cause you as the leader to take responsibility for the new role you have been given, even if it means you have to disconnect from some of those old friends and bad habits.

*Lord, I thank you for the vision to look at things*
*not based on their outward appearance as we*
*know that the eyes are design to feed the flesh,*
*but as we travel the stories of their minds, we find*
*the true desires and dreams of their hearts.*

# 7

# Don't Judge A Book By Its Cover

I am sure we have all heard this saying, but have we really looked at it from the position of leading others? Looking at someone or something by its outward appearance can be harmful later down the road. Sometimes a person could have our answer, but we never ask them the question because we were too busy looking at them from the outside instead of looking within.

Have you ever said, "I would have never guessed you would have said that?" Sure, you have, I know I have said it plenty of times, and that was because I judged the person before I ever gave them the opportunity. Another one is, have you ever wondered why they put some of the high-end places in some of the poorest areas in the city? This is because someone is looking further down the road toward the future rather than living for today. All this is saying is you are being told something by the outward perception of someone or something, but take the time to dig a little deeper. See what it is you are looking at as a whole.

In the leadership world, as a leader, you must be able to find that diamond in the rough. Your future leader is not always going to come ready to lead. As the leader, you must be able to see their potential and work to pull it out of them. Let's look at Tom Brady of the

New England Patriots. In 2000, he was drafted by the Patriots in the 6th round as the 199th overall pick. The Patriots saw a leader in Brady, and as we know, the rest is history. He has gone on to win 6 Super Bowls, which ranks him in an elite category of quarterbacks and will someday land him in the Hall of Fame.

Now I am not here to get into the whole political battle of Deflate Gate as we know it today. What I am looking at is how Bill Belichick knew Brady would become the leader he is today, because the quarterback is the heartbeat of the team. On most teams, they are normally the highest-paid person on the team, and when the team wins or loses, they're normally the first to have fingers pointed at them by the media. Under all of that, the responsibility usually falls back on the coach. While the spotlight might be on the quarterback, if something goes wrong, it's the coach who is usually fired.

My fascination still leads me back to Belichick. I don't think Brady would not have become the leader he is today without having Belichick as his coach. Now I do believe Belichick would have won Super Bowls without Brady. Why? Because Belichick is the real visionary of the team. Look at New England's team personality as a whole; it mimics Belichick's personality. The moment a player comes along and goes against it, they are normally out the door, no matter how good of a talent they are. Why? Because Belichick knows he can pull the leadership qualities out of anyone as long as they are willing to learn. That is how you are to be as a leader. You have to know you have enough confidence to pull those leadership skills out of any individual who is willing to learn, because everyone has leadership skills and qualities on the inside of them.

Leaders must be able to listen with more than just their ears, as discussed in a previous chapter. During the interview process, develop questions that a computer won't be able to answer. For example, ask the question of what time did you have to be at work on your previous job? Then later ask a second question of what time do you normally arrive at work? Depending on how these questions were answered, it tells you a lot about the person.

This tells you if the person is early, on time, or late. During my time in the Navy, I was told if I was on time, I was late; I should always be there no less than 5 minutes before the appointed time. Also, depending on the importance of the meeting, it might require me to be there at least 15 minutes prior to the start time.

From a leader's point of view, when a person is early, it lets them know that the person is serious about performing the task at hand and could later be in a role of leadership because of one of their characteristics. While the one that is on time, I still don't have a problem with them, but what happens when one of those green lights turns red or there is a note on the door saying the meeting has been moved upstairs. My on-time person now becomes a late person; it doesn't mean that their potential for leadership is not there, we just have to work on their time management. Lastly, is the late person; these actions are unacceptable, and a late person can mess the whole operation up.

That's when as a leader, you must step in and ask, "Why are you late?" Make them accountable for their actions and in time, if they get better, you know that they have the potential to become a leader one day. Based on the fact that they were willing to learn and take their job seriously, they recognized they had an issue and instead of complaining or making excuses as so many people do, they chose to make the change, and that, my friend, shows leadership quality.

During the interview process, I would not hire a late person; I would asterisk the on-time person, and I would start the early person. I categorize them this way because depending on my pool of talent, I may not have enough stars to select from, so then I fall back to those who might be a little rough around the edges. As for the late person, I am not even going to waste my time trying to discover if they are worth giving an opportunity for employment, because they said a lot to me by showing up late.

Now don't get me wrong; there are times where I might still hire a late person. That is if they have done a few things prior to being late. One, I am going to check if they called in to say, "Hey, such and such has occurred, and it is going to cause me to be late, or would you prefer that I reschedule?" When they come in, are they truly apologetic for being late? We all know when a person is genuinely sorry or when they do it based on just saying it because they think that's what you want to hear.

According to how they handle those small things would determine whether or not I completely close the door on them or give them the opportunity with an asterisk on the side of their name, but they would not receive a star. I do this because at the end of the day, we are all human, and I do believe that bad things sometimes happen to good people. Now, before bringing this type of candidate on board, I would share with them that they would have some of the stricter guidelines for a period of time based on their actions. I also would share with them that I believe in them and that they could have much success at the company, which is why I am bringing them onboard and giving them the opportunity to prove that my intuition about them was correct.

When judging a book by its cover, you are putting yourself at risk. What this risk does is put you at a disadvantage. There is nothing wrong with having a system in place that protects you from making poor decisions, and it's your system; you put it in place for your protection. As stated in the previous example, under normal circumstances, I would not be bothered nor take into consideration the candidate for the position, but based on other key factors I look at to determine if I would extend the invite to join our team.

As the leader, that decision falls back on the shoulders of me if something goes wrong, which is why I share with them that I believe in them. You never know how much a little belief in someone may carry that person further than you could ever imagine.

Another example is the movie "Pursuit of Happyness" during the part when Will Smith shows up to the interview with paint on his clothes and missing a shirt. The guy was an outstanding leader; he had previously seen something when Will put the Rubik's cube together. He knew there had to be a reason why a man would show up to an interview not looking his best when he has the intelligence to put the cube together.

He could have easily asked Mr. Smith to leave and then apologized to his supervisor for wasting his time. Instead, he stuck to his intuition, went on with the interview process, and in the end, it pays off. Sometimes the best candidate is not the right candidate. Which is why you must be able to get a feel for the person because there are things that will be said or done that the computer wouldn't pick up. As the leader, you have to understand the mission and put the right pieces of the puzzle together by not always judging a book by its cover, because doing so may very well cost you that diamond in the rough.

*Lord as we race down the runway we prepare or eyes for the unknown as we travel to new heights as we cover the Earth through your skies using your vessel. As we place ourselves back on the shelves to meditate on our successes ahead. We ask that those below us continue to record so that we have proper documentation on how successful leadership should be.*

# 8

# All Eyes Closed Aren't

# Sleep

Have you ever been in the airport and thought the person was asleep, but when they call for the plane to start boarding, the person hops up and boards the plane? It's because they weren't asleep; they were listening to what was going on. What this means is, as a leader, some of the doors that you thought were closed weren't closed; it just wasn't the time for you to walk through them. There will be times when you know that you can lead, but you won't be able to lead because there is something that you may still need to learn, and you just don't see it. People watch you and never say a word; it doesn't mean they weren't watching.

Closed eyes are wandering eyes, because there are times when you must take the time out to meditate on what is being said or done at that particular time. If you close your eyes right now in the natural, you will see either red or black. You will see these colors depending on whether you are in a room that has light or if you are in a dark space at the time.

Now take a couple of deep breaths, and what this does is relax your body and allows your brain to open up another channel of thoughts. While doing this, listen to what is happening around you. You will begin to notice things you did not notice before because you have allowed your brain to go where it needed to go to get answers that you needed for that which is at hand. I have practiced and used this technique on many occasions because before I approach my team with any information, I like to mentally process it and give it to them with clarity. A clogged mind serves as an unfiltered source of benefits. Notice the last few words of the last sentence; they were strategically placed there because I want you to allow this to soak in through the next illustration.

Imagine going to the gas pump to get gas without a pump to filter the gas to your tank. We would all be a little stunned at the thought of trying to get gas to put in our vehicle in which we need to move forward to our goal or destination. Notice at the gas pump it has a handle and a nozzle that allows the gas to easily be transported to flow to your tank from its underground holding station.

The other type of transfer of gas is having gas inside the gas can (handheld) and needing a funnel/filter to put inside the gas tank to transfer from the can to the tank. (I learned this technique as a youth when my mother would have my brothers and me mowing the lawn on the weekend. This was a great character builder for me and my brothers; we learned to work together and have responsibility at an early age.)

Let the holding station of the gas be you as the leader. Allow the processing of the information to be the filter or nozzle. While the final destination of where the gas is flowing to the tank be the recipient of the information carrying the torch to the goal. I did all of that to show the importance of the leader taking time to process the information to give to the team so they can carry out the objective.

When a leader does not take the proper steps needed to communicate a message, I promise you it will always end in disaster or in a manner they did not expect to happen. Now, earlier, I mentioned that some doors are not closed; it's just not the right time for you to go through them because there might be other information you need to learn, so don't get discouraged.

During this time, you learn another valuable skill. You learn to patiently wait. You learn to use your time wisely to meditate so that you can actively be available when the time comes for you to excel. What does this mean exactly? This means every second of your day is measured, rather than sitting and wasting what some would call free time. You take the time to gather your thoughts and ask God, "How should I use this time or what would you have me think about?"

God has a plan, although we might not know His plan for our life or every step of the way, He does. As people, we should go to our father and ask, "What will you have me learn during this time or season?" God knows what is in store for you, so before you go through that door, He wants to make sure you are prepared for what is in store for you. He does this by offering what no man can ever give you, which is true comfort, wisdom, knowledge, and strength for your journey to come. There are times when He uses other vessels to insert those things inside of you, but know it comes from Him.

Let's recap what we learned in this chapter of "All Eyes Closed Aren't Sleep." I began with the illustration of a person being in the airport with their eyes closed, with the appearance of being asleep. But when their plane calls for boarding, they pop right up to stand in line to board the plane. This was used to show people watch you even when you don't think they are watching. They are learning information about you or the task at hand. Then we learned how the leader should take the time to process the information to give to the team. Through the example of the gas tank which led to us understanding the value of a leader processing information that's given to the team. We wrapped the chapter with understanding why some doors at the time might be closed while we are going through the process of learning more information or experience for when that door opens.

*Lord as a whole we thank you as the world witnesses a new change from what we use to expect as normal, but now we all lift our heads to you the most high. Asking what would you have us to do next as you have delivered us to and through the fires of our past runways?*

# 9

# Even The President Has To Listen

No matter how high the position or title you hold, you still have to listen. Look at the President; he holds the highest position in the land, but if he fails to listen to the people, he will not be President for long. Even on their day-to-day duties, a President must listen, even if it is just to an assistant, because they have to know what they are doing for the day. The President must listen to their advisors.

They don't have to agree with what is being said, but they must listen.

When they gather the pieces for their puzzle, they know what pieces go where. For example, when a President is elected President, they are now in the position of "You Are Here but You Need to Be There." They have just taken on the job; now they need an Executive Office which they will handpick, which is "A Puzzle Has Pieces." The President, regardless of whether they are the president of the country or over a company, needs to understand that they must listen to their team. There are things going on that they may not see, but their team sees and relays the message to them, and they must put together a plan to ensure they are successful.

Let's look at the President of a company, whether big or small. They have to use the same principles and foundational tools as the managers or team leaders of the company; their decisions just carry more weight. They communicate with people like you and I (leaders). They trust that their personnel have been given the proper training, whether through continuing education (college degree) or on-the-job training (experience).

What this does is set the structure in place they need to be able to run the company efficiently and handle everyday affairs. How does a President of a large company know if what they are doing is being effective? Simple, every business is in the business for one reason and one reason only. That reason is to make a profit. You show me a business that is in business for any other reason, and I will show you a business that is nonexistent. Don't get me wrong; there are companies out there designed to just serve others, but even they need some sort of cash flow. We like to call those types of organizations charities or non-profits. Back to how they are able to tell.

They take the opportunity to look at their books. This might also be through their accounting department with those who have the proper training of running reports (balance and income statements) to communicate exactly what is going on with the company's finances. Stockholders want to know the company is making money overall because it results in them receiving dividends or having the stock price increase. This is why they invested in the company in the first place. This shows the President they are running an effective company. This, in return, means they are listening through all of those different avenues to ensure their success.

I often wondered how the President of the U.S manages to complete so many tasks throughout the day and still manages to read and stay abreast of all the current events going on in the world. I know that we have talked about putting a team together, but here I need your participation in closing your eyes and picturing a crop duster flying over the fields spraying them.

Imagine us as the fields (the people of the United States), the President as the plane and pilot, and the Executive team as the spray. Now, in the agricultural world, they spray their fields for many reasons, but I only want to highlight two for the purpose of this illustration. One is the first time they spray, which is to control the weeds that would prevent the seeds planted by the farmer (God) from growing. While the second is to control insects and eliminate harmful bacteria that could affect the harvest of the farmer who has nurtured the seeds in the fields.

Being that the President is the pilot and the plane, the Executive Team is in constant communication with Congress to keep laws in front of us (the fields) to allow us to grow to our potential harvest and not be overtaken by criminals (weeds). With the second cycle of spray, the harvest is there, but the Executive Team is in place to eliminate terrorists, whether foreign or domestic, that are trying to keep the harvest from enjoying everyday life activities.

Now, with this demonstration, the Executive Team had to work with the President in order for the people to live the American dream. What's most important is the President had to listen because it is impossible for them to be involved in every conversation that goes on in every home, every meeting going on in the boardrooms across the world (because we do have responsibilities we take care of in other countries), and still give himself the time needed to function.

I mentioned the phrase terrorists, whether foreign or domestic. Let's also add natural disasters as well. My heart goes out to every family and victim who may have lost a loved one or service member during the attacks of 9/11, Hurricane Katrina, the bombing in Boston during the parade, or even the church shooting in Charleston, SC. I know that there are more that I won't bring up during this time, but I want to prove a point. If I say I have a heart and I want to make sure that the information I have shared with you is useful so that you can apply it and use it during your everyday life. I, as the leader, then take on the responsibility to make sure I do so.

Imagine being the President of the United States during those tragic events. They have to take on the pain and the suffering for the country as we experience the loss. Can you truly imagine being in that counseling session while advice is being issued to the President on how they should handle the situation when there is no definite right way to take care of the problem?

*Lord just as the most nuclear weapons penetrates the shells of their opponents during times of war. We use ourselves as weapons of mass destruction to carry out your orders to be able to serve, provide, and protect those who fall under your command.*

# 10

# Knowing the Chain of Command

Look at Jesus, how He carried the weight of our sins on His shoulders to the cross and how He was crucified. He even asked if this could pass Him (Matthew 26:39). The next time your palm itches, I want you to imagine a nail being driven through it as was done to Jesus. I take on that thought whenever my palm itches, and I immediately say thank you, God, for your son Jesus' sacrifice.

As we review this chapter, just think about the responsibility that falls on the shoulders of the President, whether it be of the country or a company. They must have the strength to hold it all together and see their vision to the finish line for the season they are appointed to lead. Here we learned the importance of communicating with your team and listening to their feedback.

We learned this through the illustration of the President of a company being involved with the members of his team, trusting they have had the proper training along with listening to the shareholders as well. The second illustration came from the crop duster maintaining fields that allowed crops to grow into a harvest. The final illustration came with the disasters that have occurred and imagining being the President or even Jesus as He sacrificed for our sins. Although the United States of America may have its issues, at the end of the day, we are where the rest of the world wants to be.

Lastly, as leaders, remember that in order to listen to others, sometimes we may have to take care of ourselves in order to be that great leader we desire to be. Here all I am saying is to take care of your bodies both mentally and physically; otherwise, your body will make the decision to shut you down and rest. Part of being a great leader is being around to lead.

Having a chain of command shows order, but knowing who to talk to when the time comes is very important. The structure of the chain of command opens doors of opportunity for the leader to get to the right people when needed. I have been in positions when the workplace environment was designed to feel more family-oriented, which there is nothing wrong with wanting to build and have that type of work environment, as long as everyone gets along and is happy.

My issue in this environment came when needing to speak with someone; all of the roles of leadership crossed one another, so there was no real person to talk to because they would put it off on the other person who then puts it off on someone else, resulting in no real resolution. You can imagine how a person who is used to structure can become frustrated very quickly, although the people were great to be around and fun to work with.

The military is known for its structure and attention to detail. It's part of what makes it an attractive organization to be a part of. During my time in the service, I always loved the idea of knowing if I had a question or issue, there was a structured plan in place for me to reach a solution. Many people today see structure as an issue designed to hurt them.

Not us, the ones reading this book; we accept the fact that there is structure, and we use it to our advantage. Now why would I label this as strength rather than a weakness or why would it be identified as an advantage? Simple, most good leaders walk in integrity, and when walking in integrity as a leader, you put yourself under the microscope for all to see. Now what I like most about this characteristic is transparency. Once the leader shows they're honest and truly transparent, they're ready to lead.

The benefit comes into place when everyone in the chain of command has to own up to their responsibility. There are no excuses or hiding behind someone else. Your work must speak for itself because it is there for all to see. This is why I believe when you do something, no matter what it is, take pride in it and do it to the best of your ability. I never wanted to be the weakest link; I always pushed myself to add value to the team I was on or represented.

As I stated in an earlier chapter, as a leader, you must be able to show you can connect with your team and show them that you are human as well. The advantage here is the leader shows who they're accountable to. Why is this important? It's important because this allows the team to see if there is a mistake made by the leader, they have someone to go and talk to that's on their side to help get the leader back on track.

Remember, I stated earlier that a leader must be teachable. This allows them to continue to grow, but they must also be held accountable. I was taught that a person who has no one to answer to runs the risk of being a disaster or destroyer of a good opportunity. It also shows who or what the leader is responsible for. To those who are in lower positions, it shows them the levels of growth and opportunity that are available to them if they choose to proceed with climbing the ladder. But, in a different light, it shows the accountability level of that position. If something goes right or wrong, they know who is responsible.

I am sure many of you have gone into a federal building at some point in time. Here is where the government excels at maintaining the chain of command in front of people at all times. The reason I ask if you have been inside a federal building is that you will always find a picture of our President who is in office at the time. When they do that, it ties back to "A Puzzle Needs Pieces," where we spoke about the picture. It also shows that our President is at the top of the food chain. But also, on that same wall, it would show the other leaders of that building as well. This connects the members of that building to be able to see the higher-ups, while the others would know the immediate people to contact in case an issue occurred.

Imagine using two types of straws to get your drink: one with a straight straw and the second with a wraparound one with all of the turns before it reaches its destination, also known as fun or crazy straws. I use these two to represent the power of having the Chain of Command, because imagine being the straight line straw. As a person, you want to know and have direct contact with who you are trying to reach, thus the example of a straight straw. Now, allow me to clarify this statement. The straight straw allows for quickly accessing the acknowledgment of the Chain of Command. Now, I am not saying just because you know the Chain of Command, you have the right to go straight to the top of the list or jump over others just because you want a faster answer. That is unacceptable and could cause problems among the team. The person that you are jumping could feel disrespected or blindsided when approached by higher-ups about a problem that could have been solved by them and never needed to make it to the next level. During my time in the military, I ran into this sort of issue, not because I ran to the top of the chain, but because the top of the chain would come to me. I'm not saying this to pretend as if I was just the man, because that's not what I am saying at all. The person at the top of my division would come to me because I followed directions exactly as they were given to me. I illustrated earlier how I took from each of the higher-ups and did exactly what they told me to do; I didn't try to reinvent the wheel.

As a result, I gained trust, and with trust came privileges, and with privileges came problems. My team felt as if I thought I was above the system when I didn't feel that way at all; I just embraced it and used it to my advantage, at least that's what I thought. Until one day, my BM1 came to me and showed me how, although I wasn't wrong for my actions, I was just following orders, how it made them look bad as a whole. Higher-ups didn't think they knew what they were doing, while members on my level didn't respect the structure because I had special privileges. Being the team player I was, I learned to include him in the loop as a courtesy, rather than immediately going to complete the task. This, in the long run, made our division stronger.

As used earlier with the federal building, having a picture being shown gives you a clear, direct visual. While the other may come through a manual that would list the Chain of Command's order.

The second being the fun or crazy straw, causing you to go around trying to figure out who you need to contact for your resolution, thus the reason why it's going to be fun or crazy trying to figure out. I promise most people would not like this Chain of Command because frustration would set in when every time there is an issue or something needs to be resolved, nobody knows who they are to go and talk to. Kind of like me in an earlier example. From my experience, companies that have this type of structure, or should I say lack of structure, don't stay around long, or if they do manage to find a way to do so, they have to work ten times harder to stay ahead of the game.

There is actually another form of structure that could very well cause a problem as well, even if you do have all of the proper procedures in place. That form of structure is what I like to call too much structure or what some would call micro-management. This type of structure normally causes an issue because the system never allows for the individual to use their brains, that human insight that can't be calculated on a computer. As leaders, there are times we must trust our teams to know what we have taught them is on the inside of them, and we must let them act it out. Otherwise, we no longer have team members or employees of a company, but we have robots that will self-destruct, leaving us with multiple pieces to pick up.

Let's go over the highlights of this chapter that were discussed during our time together. At the beginning of this chapter, I touched on structure and how the military is one of the best at putting structure on display, whether it's directly with one of its members, as I was one of the Sailors, or if it's through pictures being shown in every federal building.

Then we went over the two straws, with one being a straight straw, which indicated the ability to have direct access to a person or a direct visual of how the system works. Lastly, I touched on the fun/crazy straw, which indicated nobody knows the order or structure, so you waste a lot of time trying to figure out how you are to get your request solved and how most companies that have this form of lack of structure normally don't stick around.

I was always taught that the fastest way to get somewhere is in a straight line. Remember, one day when you have the privilege of running your own company, if that is what you desire, having the straight line of Chain of Command will be more useful and beneficial to your company rather than the fun/crazy straw method.

*Lord we thank you as you place protection over us while being in the position we once dream and desired to be in. Your protection is greater than the treasures that are stored in the deepest parts of the ocean floors.*

# 11

# Once You Are There Stay There

It's been a journey to finally get "there," wherever your "there" may be. Some of us have bigger goals and dreams driven by a different breed of ambition. Nevertheless, you are "there," and I want to congratulate you for making it to this position, but most importantly, I want to help you stay "there." Don't get me wrong; I don't want you to believe that once you reach your destination, the journey is over, and I am encouraging you to stop and just relax and settle. I am not saying that at all because as leaders, we always strive to do better and achieve more.

What I am saying is being in the "there" position makes you vulnerable, and as leaders, we still have to work to maintain our position until we are ready to hand over the torch. Once you are "there," you will find that you will run into all sorts of issues you never imagined could exist for someone like you. Everyone likes going after the number one spot, and most importantly, they want to be the one who causes you to lose that spot, quite frankly.

Which is why earlier I stated you have to want your dreams and goals for yourself; nobody is going to work harder for you than you. People may seem as if they want the best for you, but let me be the one to break the news to you. They all have a motive, and it is up to you to determine that motive and decide how you want to channel that energy.

Being in the "there" position requires you to always be sharp and creative in order to maintain the position. There are many examples that I could share with you, but the one that stands out the most is Warren Buffett. We all know who Mr. Buffett is and his body of work, which shows the reason he has continuously maintained a position on the richest people in the world list. There was a time when Mr. Gates surpassed him, Mr. Buffett made a very interesting strategic move to regain the lead the following year. He decided to give to the Bill Gates Foundation. In doing so, Mr. Buffett practiced a different type of belief system in which I value and practice on a daily basis. That system is being a "Giver." I would have to write another book to really go into detail about sowing and reaping the benefits of your seed or the harvest of what you have sown.

As leaders, we definitely need to practice this principle on a daily basis because it is part of who we are as leaders, whether it is for our companies, families, or our communities. You can never go wrong with giving of your time, talent, or treasure unless it comes from an unhealthy position, but if you practice being a cheerful giver (2 Corinthians 9:7), you put yourself in a position to receive more. If you are not using this principle, I strongly suggest that you start at the level you are on.

As leaders, and for the purpose of this book, you could start by mentoring someone underneath you and being openly transparent with them. By being openly transparent, I mean being upfront and honest about how you got to the position you are in. Talk to them and explain the steps you took, whether or not

they were the proper ones to take. Now, this is not a conversation you have with everyone, but for those individuals you see who have the potential and are hungry enough to learn. I have shared with you the importance and the value of time. You wouldn't just throw seed on ground that is unworthy of producing the harvest you desire. No, you are going to place your seed in a place that is going to receive the proper amount of sunlight and water needed to produce a harvest down the line.

This system works, especially if you plan on moving up. Mind you, this is not done in hopes that the person above you decides to take the time out to start mentoring you because you don't know if they are willing or want to give you their position. You practice this because it allows you to open the door for God to work through others to work with you. I need you to practice this daily because eventually I want you to be able to receive from unknown resources at any given time.

I apologize in advance for those who may feel I got off subject, but I have a very strong passion about giving and being a servant. That was for those of us who have a passion for being a leader and taking it seriously and allowing God to move you to your "there" position.

Back to Mr. Buffett, during that time, he wasn't ready to give up his "there" position. Although I have never met Mr. Buffett, I respect his mind for business as well as his heart for giving. Along with his ability to stay in his "there" position for such a long period of time. You never hear about him in the news for making unethical transactions just to get ahead. Mr. Buffett is also a perfect example of "Walking the Line and Not Crossing It." As a result, he is one of those leaders people look up to and want to be like, as well as a leader who knows God will protect him for the work he has done.

As I stated earlier in this chapter, being in the "There" position leaves us in a vulnerable position. I included this because all of us who have worked hard to get to the "There" position, and those who are in the process of getting there, work hard to achieve our level of success. Make no mistake, when you are an eagle, you hang and surround yourself with other eagles. You will not find an eagle hanging out in a chicken coop, but with other eagles because iron sharpens iron (Proverbs 27:17).

This chapter was placed at the end of the book, not by accident but by choice, because I wanted to go on the journey with you. Every bit of information I have given thus far has been given to you to encourage the journey of getting to the "There" position, whether o r not I said it through an illustration or through direct communication. I said it to paint a picture, to draw on that sense of being there with you or you being alongside me. I did it to be a storyteller for you to share with your team. Being "There" you never know how important it is until you are no longer "There," especially if it was taken away from you and not willingly turned over. Being "There" gives you the opportunity to give back. The opportunity is there because just like my experience with my individual earlier, who turned out to be a motivator, your audience will listen to you based on your position.

If you were to take all of the past chapters and combine them all together, you should see how by now you should have a feel for your position. You should have an understanding of how every position works, whether below or above your position. You should also be able to identify with your team members as to what motivates them and what direction they are headed in. Lastly, you should be able to identify with the "There" position because you have made it to this point in the book. I can honestly say that being in the "There" position is truly a blessing and offers a sense of fulfillment.

*Lord we show gratitude towards you as we close the*
*pages of a crowned jewel that has changed our lives.*
*Which in returned will change the lives of many*
*others as we go out and apply what you have*
*allowed to be stored within us to take root.*

# Ending Statement

Now that you have completed the journey of reading "The Do What You Are Told Leader," I wanted to leave you with some thoughts of encouragement. As a leader, always commit to doing what is right. Be aware when you face new beginnings. Make decisions in accordance with the vision, as they are the ones with the vision. Take the time to look for those diamonds in the rough; they usually yield big dividends. Don't forget the moments that sparked your drive to want more. Make sure not to automatically assume the unknown. Watch for those who appear not to have interest. Being at the top doesn't mean you are not required to listen and follow directions. Having an understanding of position and power gives you an advantage. As leaders, once you are at your desired destination or goal, take the opportunity to enjoy your achievement and continue to find ways to improve. Stay in the mindset of learning. I hope all of you have found something that you can use from this reading and apply it to your daily lives, and remember when it comes time to lead, simply Do What You Are Told.

# About the Author

Shagdrick Hill is a devoted believer in Jesus Christ and a loving father to two wonderful daughters, who have both played a pivotal role in shaping him into the person he is today. With a profound belief in fulfilling God's calling to serve His people, Shagdrick aspires to lead by example and inspire others to realize their life ambitions.

A proud veteran of the US Navy, Shagdrick's dedication extends beyond military service. In his leisure time, he derives immense satisfaction from actively participating in community service initiatives. His multifaceted experiences and unwavering commitment to making a positive impact on others have made him a source of inspiration for those around him.

Shagdrick Hill's life journey is a testament to his belief in service, love for his family, and dedication to his faith. Through his words and actions, he continues to uplift and empower others, encouraging them to reach their full potential.

Made in the USA
Middletown, DE
30 October 2023

41668301R00070